The Cooking Queen's

Life is Delicious

Cookbook

To Rachel,
"Life is Delicious"
Linda Ogden Epling

The Cooking Queen's *Life is Delicious* Cookbook

Linda Ogden Epling

Photography by Paul Marcellini

LOE Publishing, Inc. Weston, Florida

Acknowledgments

This book is again a work from my heart! Thank you to my family and dear friends for their love, support and prayers for this book.

To Paul Marcellini, I appreciate your creative photographic talent. Your vision for light, texture and design took it to another level. Your kind spirit and genuine love of photography made this book a pleasure to write!

To sweet Jackie Brown of Hirni's Wayside Garden Florist, a special thank you for your visual and artistic design with flowers and color. You are truly a gifted, creative, and wonderful friend.

To my friend Ginny DeBoliac, who once again worked hard and tirelessly by my side, encouraging and supporting me with the text, photo shoots and layout. I thank you sincerely for making me do it right! You made us laugh!!

To Mary Beth Horton, a dear true friend and an "English Grammarian". I thank you for your dedication, wisdom, wealth of knowledge and constant encouragement to me.

To my sister, Anita Jenkins and my friend, Bonnie Court. Thank you for the second "set of eyes" that helped the book flow smoothly. You made the photo shoots such fun! Your praise and encouragement were wonderful.

To my lifetime friend, Stacy Lohr, thank you for your hard work with the text. I so appreciate your encouragement and support.

To Nancy Quinones and Frankie Ferguson, thank you for your input, advice and support for titles, text and design. I appreciate you both.

To Andrew Ogden and Monique and Adam Ogden, thank you for the use of your beautiful homes, in which we photographed several segments of this book.

To Ashley and Christie Ogden, my profound gratitude for your intricate legal guidance in the production of this book.

To Hirni's Wayside Garden Florist, for your perfect and beautiful location. Thank you for your amazing staff who helped pull it together!

To Cauley Square, for your beautiful and spooky setting. Thank you for being so generous and helpful.

To Burr's Berry Farm and family, you made your location a perfect chapter for the book. You are wonderful, cherished, lifetime friends!

Photography by Paul Marcellini - Crown Logo Design by Richard McKee

Design and Layout Cowen Design Inc., Miami, Florida
Contact publisher LOE Publishing, Inc. at www.loepublishing.com
First Edition 2012 ISBN 978-0-615-65727-1. Proudly printed by Global Print Services, Inc.

Contents

Introduction

A motto that I believe in or try to live by is that when life gives you lemons, "Make Lemon Meringue Pie!" When life gave me lemons, I published my first cookbook, "*The Cooking Queen Opens Her Kitchen*" in 2009.

Through my travels with this book, I was inspired with a new thought, "Life is Delicious." I have enjoyed meeting many new friends and readers as I have shared my cookbook. I have heard repeatedly that the recipes provide wonderful ideas for cooking, decorating and entertaining. Large print, user friendly recipes, wipeable paper and pictures that allow you to actually see what you are cooking have been enjoyed by all. Enticing food menus with scrumptious pictures of the food are sure to set your mood for any occasion.

We are all given special gifts and talents from God. I am thankful for my talents in cooking and entertaining that He has gifted me to share with you.

All of this has kept one thought in my mind and I am happy to use it as the title of my new book, "*The Cooking Queen's Life is Delicious Cookbook.*"

-Linda

Trousseau Tea

A "Trousseau Tea" is an old-fashioned tea party that helps the bride to gather, enjoy and display gifts received from her family and friends. Afternoon lite-fare of sweets and goodies are served with tea, punch and perhaps, bubbly. You will want your tea for her to be a very memorable day in her life. I have shared this party with many family members and their friends, hosting this joyous event for the bride-to-be. We hope these ideas will make elegant memories for your invited guests and keepsakes for the bride.

Menu

Elegant Sandwich Loaf on Tray with Rose Petals

Assorted Fresh Fruit Tray with Orange Marshmallow Crème Dip

Mini Tomato Pies in Pastry Shells

Pecan Toasted Stuffed Dates

Spicy Cheese Crispy

Desserts

Sugared Tea Cakes

Happily Ever After Cookies

Brides' Blonde Brownie

Beverages

Brides' Punch

Queen's Tips

Use a decorated parasol for the gift table centerpiece. Fresh flowers cascading on the handle of the parasol and beautiful bridal ribbons tied to match are oh, so pretty! Fresh rose petals also add to the elegance of the food and table.

Use your best silver, crystal and china for this special occasion. A beautiful table is always an eye catcher!

Serve a cake or cookies that say, "Happily Ever After." Everyone will send her off with this special thought!

Recipes

Elegant Sandwich Loaf

1 loaf Pullman Bread
(May be purchased at local bakery.)
1 container whipped margarine

Egg Salad Filling

Mix the following ingredients for egg salad filling and set aside.
10 chopped hard cooked eggs
4 tablespoons sweet pickle relish, drained
4 heaping tablespoons mayonnaise
¼ teaspoon salt
Few grains pepper

Ham Filling

Mix the following ingredient for ham filling and set aside.
3 cups ground cooked ham, or turkey ham (I use turkey ham.)
1 heaping teaspoon grainy mustard
½ cup mayonnaise

Chicken-Salad Filling

Mix the following ingredients for chicken salad filling and set aside.
6 boneless, skinless chicken breasts
½ cup celery, finely chopped and drained
½ teaspoon salt
1 cup dried cranberries
1 cup mayonnaise
¼ cup honey
Fresh parsley for garnish

Boil chicken breasts, cool and dice. Add chopped celery, salt and cranberries to diced chicken. Blend together mayonnaise and honey. Combine all ingredients.

Slice loaf lengthwise in four slices with knife or have the baker slice with bread slicer. Remove crust from bread. Spread both sides of each slice with whipped margarine.

Then, spread the first slice, butter side up with chicken salad filling; place second slice of bread on top and cover with egg filling; place third slice of bread on top and cover with ham filling. Top with fourth slice of bread.

Combine:
4 (8 oz.) cream cheese
½ cup of light whipping cream
Add more whipping cream, if needed, until cream cheese reaches spreading consistency. Beat until soft and fluffy. Spread cream cheese generously on top and sides like you are frosting a cake. Decorate with fresh flowers or petals.

Assorted Fresh Fruit Tray

1 quart whole fresh strawberries
4 cups fresh pineapple chunks
3 clusters whole green grapes
Fresh mint for garnish

Wash fruit and arrange on tray. Serves 8.
TIP: I like to garnish tray with fresh flowers!

Orange Marshmallow Crème

1 (8 oz.) package cream cheese
1 (7 oz.) jar marshmallow crème
2 tablespoons orange juice

Mix together and spoon a dollop on individual servings of fruit.

Mini Tomato Pie

Pastry Shells

1 package ready-made pie crust rolls

Roll open and cut with round cookie cutter. Press into ungreased mini-muffin pans.

Filling

6 red tomatoes, chopped
4 fresh basil leaves, chopped
1 cup sour cream
1 cup mayonnaise
1 ½ cups shredded Cheddar cheese

Combine all ingredients and fill pastry shells with a heaping teaspoon of mixture. Bake at 400 degrees for 15 minutes. Reduce heat to 350 degrees for 10 minutes. Cool slightly. Serves 8.

Pecan Toasted Stuffed Dates

1 (10 oz.) box pitted whole dates
1 (8oz.) package cream cheese
1 cup pecans
Cherry juice (enough to be smooth, not thin)

Combine cherry juice with cream cheese. Mix until smooth. Split dates lengthwise and fill with cheese. Top with a toasted pecan.

(See "We All Love Fall" for the toasted almond recipe.)

Spicy Cheese Crispy

8 oz. sharp cheddar cheese, shredded
1 stick unsalted butter
1 cup all-purpose white flour
1 teaspoon crushed red pepper
1 cup crispy rice cereal (I use Rice Krispies™.)

Cream cheddar cheese and butter until well-mixed. Sift dry ingredients and add cheese mixture. Fold in cereal. Refrigerate dough overnight. Roll into small balls, and flatten with a wet fork. Bake at 350 degrees for 12 to 15 minutes on ungreased cookie sheet. Makes about 18.

Desserts

Sugared Tea Cakes

1 cup shortening
1 ½ cups white sugar
1 egg
1 teaspoon vanilla or lemon extract
2 cups self-rising white flour

Cream the first 4 ingredients, and combine with flour until blended. Roll into small balls, flatten slightly. Bake at 350 degrees for 10 minutes. Makes 20 to 24.

Happily Ever After Cookies

Dough

4 cups all-purpose white flour
2 cups unsalted butter
4 egg yolks, slightly beaten
1 cup dairy sour cream

Place flour in large bowl. With pastry blender, cut in butter until mixture resembles coarse crumbs. Add egg yolks and sour cream; stir until combined. Turn out on lightly floured surface and knead until dough is smooth and can be shaped into a ball. If the dough is too sticky, add in more flour.

Filling

1 ¼ pounds walnuts, ground
1 cup white sugar
½ cup whole milk
1 tablespoon almond extract
1 egg, beaten
Confectioners' sugar

In medium bowl, combine nuts, white sugar, milk and almond extract; blend well.

Preheat oven to 400 degrees. Grease cookie sheets. On lightly floured surface, roll out ¼ of dough at a time, to 1/8 inch thick or thicker. With a pastry wheel or knife, cut into 2 inch squares.

Place a generous ½ teaspoon filling in center of each square, and bring together opposite corners, overlapping filling: pinch edges with a fork to seal. Arrange on cookie sheets. Brush lightly with egg.

Bake 10 to 12 minutes, or until golden. Remove and roll in confectioners' sugar. Allow to cool. (Must be stored in refrigerator.) *They are just so good!*

Desserts

Brides' Blonde Brownies

1 ½ sticks of butter, melted and cooled
3 eggs, beaten
1 pound of light brown sugar
2 ½ cups self-rising white flour
1 (12 oz.) package chocolate chips
1 cup pecans, chopped

Mix butter, eggs, sugar, and flour until well-blended. Fold in pecans and chocolate chips. Bake in a lightly greased 9 x 13 inch pan at 325 degrees for 30 minutes. Cut into circles or squares. Makes 2 dozen.

1 (12 oz.) can frozen orange juice
1 (6 oz.) can frozen lemonade
1 cup sugar
2 cups strong tea
1 (46 oz.) can pineapple juice
1 quart ginger ale

Mix chilled ingredients in a punch bowl. Float orange slices and fresh mint on top for garnish. Serves 20.

Optional:

Flavored Tea of Choice

Iced Lemon Water

All About Hearts

Hearts, flowers, chocolates and someone special to love! Valentine's Day is a wonderful time to combine colors of red and pink. Heart-shaped dishes, rose petals, and a delicious, decadent dessert for your special someone is what makes this day memorable.

Menu

Chicken Breasts with Raspberry Sauce and Fresh Raspberry Garnish
Marinated Herbed Lamb Chops
Broccoli Casserole
Red Pepper Rice
Tomato Aspic in Heart - Shaped Mold

Breads

Heart-Shaped Chive Biscuits with Heart-Shaped Flavored Butters
Strawberry Bread
Chocolate Double Fudge Muffins

Desserts

Chocolate Chip Marble Pie with White Chocolate Garnish
Carolyn's Decadent Strawberry Dessert

Beverages

Cranberry Spritz
Pink Champagne Punch
Wine of Choice

Queen

Make sure the marinade is done in plenty of time to allow flavors to blend.

To dress up muffin arrays, use ribbons on serving platters and trays, in shapes and in colors of your theme.

Try a cupcake stand to display muffin varieties. Remember to include fresh rose petals for your romantic table.

Mini ice heart molds make even your drinks festive for your guests.

Tips

Mix and match different containers for flowers and arrangements.

Remember everything looks better with a variety of colors and flowers that match your holiday.

"Don't forget," lighted candles give an intimacy to a table that is hard to equal, with any other decorations! Consider their height carefully. Candles should stand above the line of vision across the table, so as not to glare in one's eyes.

Recipes

Tomato Aspic in Heart-Shaped Mold

2 cups tomato juice (or vegetable juice)
1 (3 oz.) package of lemon Jell-O™
1 cup celery, chopped

Heat tomato juice (or vegetable juice). Add to lemon Jell-O™ powder. Dissolve. Add chopped celery. Pour in mold and chill. Serve with a cream dressing on top or side. Add a dollop of sour cream and chopped chives for garnish.

Heart-Shaped Chive Biscuits

2 cups self-rising flour
1 cup buttermilk
2/3 cup shortening
½ cup chopped chives
½ cup Cheddar cheese, grated

Sift flour; make a well in center of flour. Add shortening to well and pour buttermilk over shortening and mix. Stir in cheddar cheese and chives. Pat out on floured board and cut with heart shaped cutter. Bake in greased pan at 450 degrees for 20 minutes. Makes about 10 biscuits.

Tip: Put a dab of icing on cake plate to hold the cake on the plate when frosting.

Chicken Breast with Rasberry Sauce

6 to 8 boneless, skinless chicken breasts
2 cups Italian salad dressing
2 cups bread crumbs (plain or Italian)
1 cup shredded Swiss cheese

Wash chicken; pat dry. Marinate overnight (or at least 2 hours) in Italian salad dressing. Drain chicken. Dredge chicken on both sides in bread crumbs and Swiss cheese that have been blended together. Place breasts in a lightly greased 9 x 13 inch pan and bake uncovered at 350 degrees for 1 hour. Serve with Raspberry Sauce and fresh raspberries on top. Serves 6 to 8.

Raspberry Sauce

1 cup water
¼ cup white sugar
2 tablespoon cornstarch
1 (10 oz.) package frozen raspberries, thawed, not drained

Combine water, sugar and cornstarch in a saucepan. Cook, stirring constantly until thick and clear. Stir in raspberries. Spoon over chicken and serve.

Marinated Lamb Chops

4 to 6 Lamb or Veal Chops, marinated for 1 hour or overnight in a Ziploc™ bag with:
1 teaspoon crushed red pepper
1 teaspoon salt
1 teaspoon fresh oregano, chopped
3 tablespoon green olives
2 garlic cloves, chopped
Zest of 1 whole lemon
Juice of 1 whole lemon

After marinating:
Sauté lamb chops in 1 tablespoon of olive oil for 3 minutes on the first side and 2 minutes on the second side. Timing is important!

Then, add ½ cup water to cover and cook 1 minute. Turn off fire and cover to keep warm.

Serve on platter with fresh oregano, whole green olives and tomato rose.

Broccoli Casserole

2 packages frozen chopped broccoli or 2 large bunches of fresh broccoli, chunked
1 egg, beaten
1 cup Cheddar cheese, grated
1 small onion, finely chopped
½ cup mayonnaise
1 can cream of mushroom soup
Salt and pepper to taste
½ sleeve of crackers, crushed

Cook broccoli until tender and drain. Place broccoli in casserole dish, and add all other ingredients reserving ½ cup of the cheese and crackers. Stir and sprinkle remaining cheese on top. Crumble crackers on the top and bake for 50 to 60 minutes at 350 degrees. Allow casserole to rest for 10 minutes before serving. Serves 6.

Red Pepper Rice

1 cup uncooked white rice
2 ½ cups chicken broth
½ teaspoon salt
1/8 teaspoon pepper
¾ cup red pepper, chopped
¾ cup green onion, chopped
¼ cup parsley, chopped
¼ cup butter
1 (8 oz.) can water chestnuts, drained and sliced (optional)

Combine rice, chicken broth, salt, and pepper in a medium saucepan; cover and cook over medium heat 20 minutes or until done. Set rice aside and keep warm. Sauté pepper, green onion, and parsley in butter; stir into rice. If desired, stir in water chestnuts. Yields 6 servings.

Breads

Strawberry Bread

3 cups white all-purpose flour
1 teaspoon baking soda
1 teaspoon salt
1 tablespoon cinnamon
2 cups white sugar
4 eggs, beaten
1 ¼ cup pecans or walnuts, chopped
2 cups frozen strawberries, thawed

Mix all dry ingredients using a hand mixer. Add all other ingredients until well-combined. Pour into 2 greased loaf pans. Bake at 350 degrees for 60 minutes or until tester comes out clean. Makes 2 loaves.

Chocolate Double Fudge Muffins

4 blocks semi-sweet chocolate
1 cup melted margarine
½ teaspoon salt
1 cup white sugar
1 cup all-purpose white flour
4 eggs
1 teaspoon vanilla extract
2 cups walnuts or pecans, chopped

Melt margarine and chocolate in pan. Cool slightly. Beat in sugar, salt and flour. Add eggs, one at a time, then vanilla and nuts. Pour into greased (or papered) muffin pans. Bake at 325 degrees for 25 minutes. Dust with powdered sugar. Makes 12 muffins.

Desserts

Chocolate Chip Marble Pie with White Chocolate Garnish

2 eggs
½ cup all-purpose white flour
½ cup white sugar
½ cup brown sugar, firmly packed
1 cup butter melted and cooled to room temperature
1 (6 oz.) bag semisweet chocolate chips
1 cup chopped walnuts (optional)
9 inch pie crust, uncooked
Whipped topping or ice cream (optional)

Beat eggs until fluffy. Add flour, sugar and brown sugar. Blend well. Add butter and blend. Stir in chocolate chips and nuts. Pour into pie crust. (See Quick Pie Crust Pastry recipe.) Bake pie in 325 degree oven for 50 minutes to 1 hour (or until set). Serve warm with preferred topping.

1 cup flour
1/3 cup shortening
1/4 teaspoon salt
3 tablespoons ice water

Cut shortening into flour and salt, until crumbly. Add water. Stir just until moistened. Roll out crust on floured board to fit the pie plate with extra around edge and place in pie plate. Using knife, cut around edge of pie plate cutting off excess dough mixture. Crimp the edge.

Carolyn's Strawberry Dessert

1 large angel food cake
1 large package strawberry Jell-O™
3 cups water
1 large package frozen strawberries or 2 cups fresh sliced strawberries
1 large package instant vanilla pudding
3 cups whole milk
1 cup pecans, chopped
1 large whipped topping

Tear angel food cake into pieces and place in a 9 x 13 inch pan. Mix Jell-O™, using 3 cups warm water. Pour over cake pieces. Add strawberries and pecans on top of this. Mix instant pudding according to package directions using 3 cups of milk. Pour over strawberries. Top with whipped topping. Refrigerate for at least 2 hours before serving. Delicious and easy! Serves 8.

Tip: Remember to garnish your trays and dishes with the freshest of herbs from the garden!

Beverages

Cranberry Spritz

1 (24 oz.) bottle Cranapple Juice
1 liter bottle Ginger Ale
Mix ingredients in punch bowl and serve.

Pink Champagne Punch

1 bottle Pink Champagne
2 (24 ounce) bottles White Grape Juice
1 (2 liter) Ginger Ale
1 (2 liter) Lemon Lime Soda
2 clusters red grapes, frozen

Mix ingredients in punch bowl and chill.
Float frozen red grapes on top and serve. Serves 20.

Optional: Wine of Choice

That's So Cheesy

Let me introduce your next party of connoisseurs to a great companion: the wonderful world of cheese. Let's journey through an array of cheeses and discover tasty pairing that will make your party festive and successful for all to enjoy. This chapter will inspire you to be "cheese-a-licious"!

Menu

Tray of Brie Cheese
- Brie
- Camembert

Tray of Blue Cheese
- Maytag
- Roquefort

Tray of Hard Cheese
- Asiago
- Gouda
- Premoo Gouda
- Manchego

Tray of Chèvre Cheese
- Cranberry
- Herb
- Cranberry Cinnamon
- Pepper

Tray of Cheddar Cheese
- Cheddar Sharp
- Monterey Jack
- White Sharp Cheddar
- Port Wine Cheese Ball
- Hot Cheese Fondue

Appropriate fruits, crackers and breads shown are with cheese of choice.

Napa Valley Reserve
N37-6
STORAGE BARRE
CAP 59 GAL
GOUDA
BERINGER
TWO VINES

Make sure you use a variety of assorted trays and boards that look and match the color of your cheese choices. Examples would be: Blue cheese that pops on a marble tray and hard cheese looks and slices well on a wooden board. Try not to cube cheese, try breaking it into small bite-size pieces. Mark or label your trays in order for guests to know the varieties that they are enjoying. Buy bold and interesting cheeses that will light up your palate. Garnish the cheese boards with leaves, fruit or fresh herbs of the season.

Brie

Brie is a semi-soft gooey cheese with a white surface rind. It is delicious served cold or warmed with an apricot or strawberry glaze. Brie is lovely with a sprinkle of slivered almonds or pecans on top. If you like a mild cheese, you will enjoy these.

Camembert

Camembert – soft and gooey, also slightly stronger than Brie

Suggested fruits that accompany Brie and Camembert:
- Apricots
- Green grapes
- Red and green apple slices

Suggested breads and crackers:
- Bread Sticks
- French Baguette

Suggested Wines:
- Pinot Noir
- Merlot
- Beaujolais

Blue Cheese

Blue Cheeses are sharp and salty. Maytag Blue and Roquefort have a similar appearance. Cambozola Blue has a creamy cheese texture and very strong bite.

Roquefort Blue

Roquefort Blue is the sharpest and saltiest of the "Blues". It is a famous sheep's milk cheese from Southern France. Blue Stilton is crumbly and best served on salads. If you enjoy sharp cheese you will like the salty Blues.

- Maytag Blue
- Roquefort
- Gorgonzola
- Blue Stilton

Suggested fruits for Blue Cheeses:
- Apple slices
- Purple grapes
- Champagne Grapes
- Caper Berries
- Pears

Suggested breads and crackers:
- Whole wheat crackers or oat crackers
- Blue Chips or Walnut Bread

Suggested Wines:
- Sauterne
- Chardonnay

Hard Cheeses

Hard Cheeses are hard because they contain less liquid than other cheeses and are more firm than most; also included are Swiss, Gruyere and Parmesan.

Asiago
Gouda
Premoo Gouda
Manchego

Manchego

Manchego is a semi-hard sheep's cheese. Men seem to love this cheese.

Suggested fruits and accompaniments that go well with these cheeses are:
- Capers
- Black olives
- Greek peppers or pepperoncini
- Salami-peppered
- Prosciutto with mozzarella roll
- Spicy Mustard

Suggested breads and crackers:
- Table Water Crackers
- Asiago Bread broken into small servings

Red wine goes well with these cheeses. Sherry or Tawny Port are options.

Chèvre Cheese

Chèvre Cheese is also known as Goat cheese. This is a type of French cheese made from goat's milk. With a relatively sharp taste, Chèvre is often paired with herbs and fruits.

Cranberry Chèvre
- Herb Chèvre
- Cranberry Cinnamon Chèvre
- Pepper Chèvre

Suggested fruits for Chèvre Cheese:
- Green grapes
- Kiwi
- Cranberries

Suggested breads and crackers:
- Mini Petite plain crackers
- Rosemary crackers
- Walnut bread or raisin bread broken into bite size pieces

Suggested Wines:
- Rosé
- Riesling

Cheddar

Cheddar cheese is a cow's milk cheese that is relatively hard, pale yellow to off white and sometimes sharp tasting. Cheddar cheese originated in England and is popular for snacking. It is often used melted for sauces and cooking.

Cheddar Sharp
Monterey Jack
White Sharp Cheddar
Linda's Port Wine Cheese Ball
Hot Cheese Fondue

Suggested fruits for Cheddar:
- Apples
- Strawberries
- Red or green grapes

Suggested bread or crackers:
- French bread rounds, toasted
- Focaccia Pesto Bread
- Cheese Straws
- Bread Sticks

Recipes

Linda's Port Wine Cheese Ball

2 (8 ounce) packages cream cheese, softened
2 cups Cheddar cheese shredded
1 stick of butter
2 teaspoons horseradish
1 tablespoon fresh chives, chopped
1 cup nuts, chopped
¼ to ½ cup Port Wine

Mix all ingredients until well-blended and form into a ball. Roll in nuts. Chill and serve with fresh fruit or crackers.

Hot Cheese Fondue

1 pound Velveeta™ cheese
2 cups shredded Cheddar cheese
1 (10 oz. can) diced tomatoes with green chilies
3 green onions, chopped
½ teaspoon hot sauce

Melt cheese in microwave.
Add diced tomatoes, green onions and hot sauce.
Serve hot with taco chips.

Fresh from th

Garden, Soups and Salads

Growing up, our family has always loved cooking and serving the freshest of fruits and vegetables in our home. This is a tradition I continue with my family and guests. Using the freshest ingredients provides the opportunity to serve healthy "Soups and Salads, Fresh from the Garden," just like Mom!

Menu

Soups

Ham and White Bean Soup

French Onion Soup

Roasted Red Pepper and Tomato Soup

Cheddar Potato Soup

Salads

Cornbread Salad

Chattanooga Salad

Lime Drizzle Dressing

Tomato Cucumber Salad

Strawberry Field Green Salad

Bread

Corn Muffins

Biscuits

Desserts

Heavenly Pecan Pie

Old -Fashioned Rice -Raisin Pudding

*Tip: Any of the above salads
an be accompanied
with chicken, salmon or shrimp.*

Placing a dish cloth under your cutting board prevents your board from moving on your counter when slicing ingredients. Serving your soups in a bread bowl makes cleaning up easier on the cook. Fresh herbs enhance flavors as do mixing fruits with vegetables.

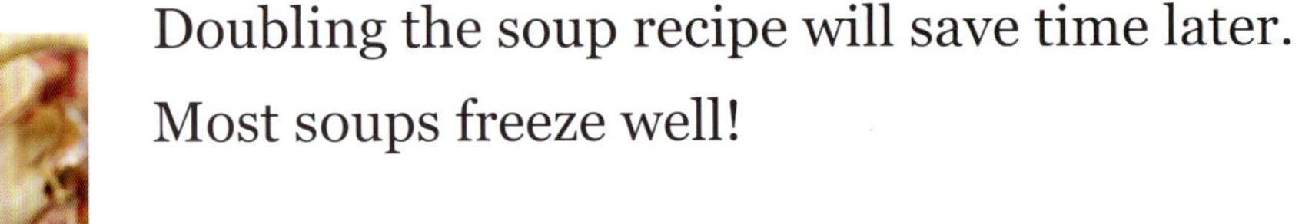

Doubling the soup recipe will save time later. Most soups freeze well!

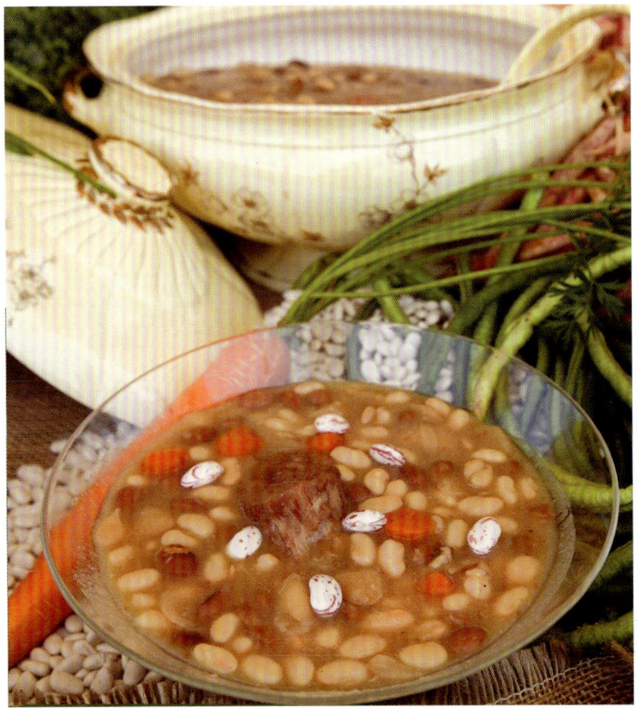

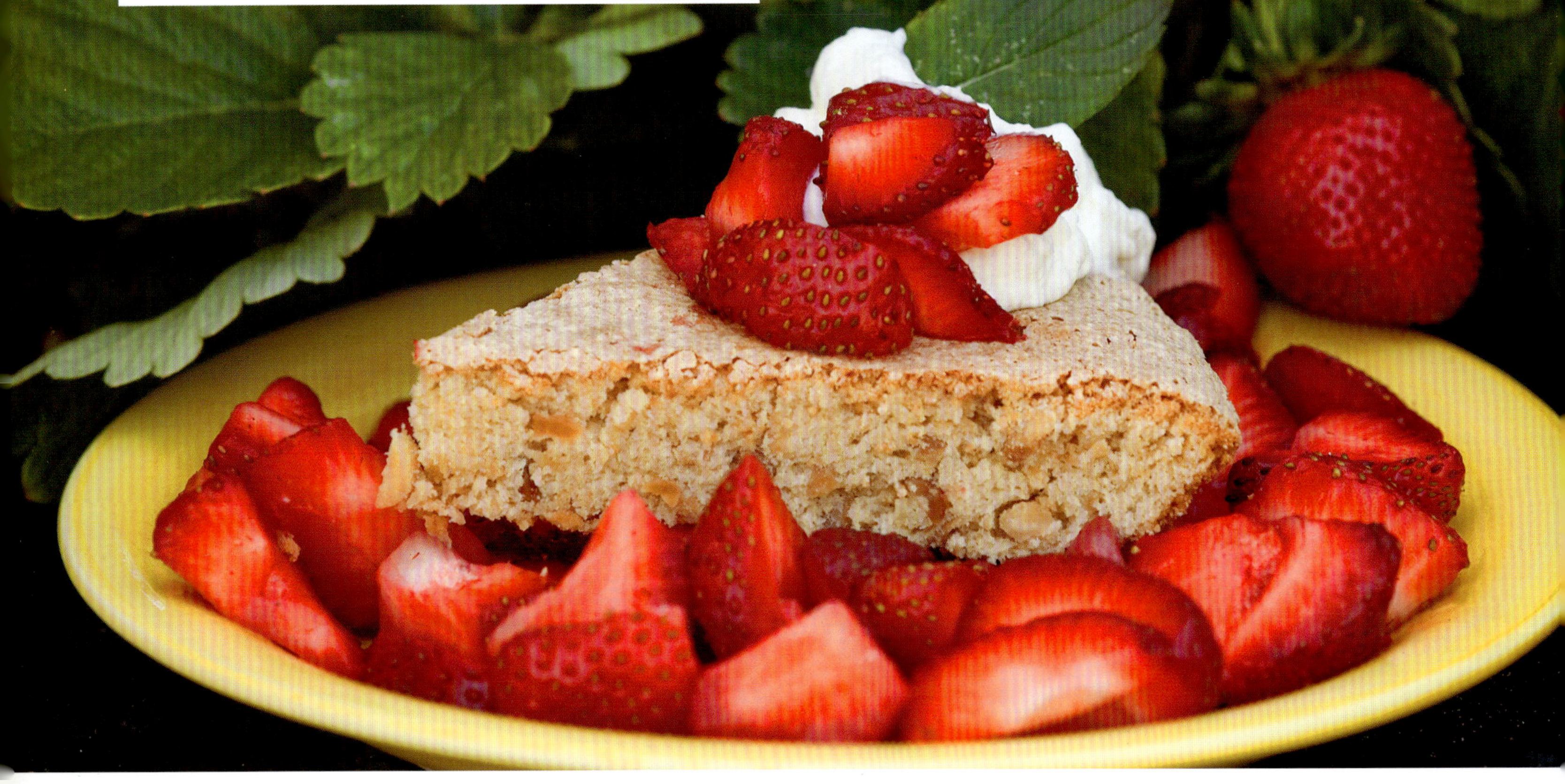

COLD

Recipes

Soups

Ham and White Bean Soup

1 ham bone or 1 turkey bone or 1 ½ cups cubed ham chunks
1 ½ cups dried navy beans, soaked overnight or 3 cans navy beans drained
1 medium onion, chopped
3 stalks celery, chopped
2 large bay leaves
1 teaspoon salt
1 teaspoon pepper
6 cups water

Combine all ingredients and simmer for 3 hours or until beans are soft. Best served with good ole' cornbread or buttermilk biscuits. Serves 10.

French Onion Soup

4 to 6 large sweet onions, peeled and sliced thin
6 tablespoons butter
5 cups beef broth
1 cup chicken broth
½ teaspoon sugar
2 cloves garlic, crushed
Dash of Sherry
Grated Gruyère cheese
6 slices toasted French bread rounds

Sauté onion and garlic in butter until translucent; add sugar. Add broth and bring to boil. Simmer 30 to 40 minutes. Add sherry. Place toasted French bread rounds in individual soup ramekins or bread bowls. Ladle onion soup on top of bread. Grate cheese on top. Bake in a 350 degree oven until cheese melts. Serves 6.

Roasted Red Pepper and Tomato Soup

2 teaspoons light olive oil
1 white onion, chopped fine
2 cloves garlic, minced
1 jar (12 oz.) roasted red bell peppers in water, drained and chopped
4 large tomatoes, peeled and chopped
½ teaspoon white sugar
6 cups chicken broth
1 teaspoon hot sauce
2 tablespoons butter
2 tablespoons flour
Salt and pepper to taste

Heat the oil and sauté onion and garlic until soft. Add tomatoes, bell peppers, sugar, broth, hot sauce, salt and pepper. Simmer on low for 20 minutes covered. Strain solids from broth, reserving broth. Process solids in a food processor until smooth. Add purée to reserved broth. Melt butter, stir in flour, and add to soup. Simmer for 15 minutes. Season to taste. Serve in a bowl with 1 tablespoon of sour cream on top and garnish with fresh basil. Serves 6.

Cheddar Potato Soup

2 cups chicken broth
4 cups peeled red potato cubes
6 tablespoon butter
1 medium onion, chopped
6 tablespoons all-purpose flour
1 teaspoon pepper
3 cups whole milk
3 cups light cream
1 teaspoon sugar
2 cups Cheddar cheese
2 cups cubed cooked ham (optional)

Bring chicken broth to a boil in a large pot. Add potatoes and cook until tender. Drain potatoes reserving broth. Melt butter, add onions, and cook until tender, not browned. Add flour and pepper. Gradually add potatoes, reserved broth, milk, cream, sugar to onion mixture; stir well. Add cheese (ham optional). Simmer on low heat for 30 minutes, stirring often. Serves 12. TIP: I like to garnish with grated Cheddar cheese and a sprig of fresh herbs.

Salads

Cornbread Salad

1 (12 oz.) package cornbread
½ cup sweet pickle relish chunks
½ cup sweet pickle juice
1 pint cherry tomatoes cut in half
½ package bacon, fried and crumbled
1 bell pepper, chopped
1 cup mayonnaise

Cook cornbread as directed on package. Cool. Crumble cornbread and add all other ingredients. Stir lightly to combine. Serves 6 to 8.

Chattanooga Salad

6 fresh peaches, sliced with skin on, or strawberries sliced
6 ounces fresh baby Mozzarella cheese, cut into bite size pieces
4 teaspoon fresh chopped basil

Arrange peaches or strawberry slices on a small platter or plate. Place Mozzarella cheese chunks on top and drizzle with lime dressing. Garnish with basil on top. Delicious. Serves 6 to 8.

Lime Drizzle

4 tablespoons salad oil
4 tablespoons honey
1 teaspoon grated lime peel
4 teaspoons fresh lime juice

Mix together and drizzle over peach or strawberry salad.

Tomato Cucumber Salad

6 tomatoes
4 cucumbers
Italian salad dressing of choice
Salt and pepper to taste
Fresh herbs of choice

Slice and arrange on tray. Drizzle Italian salad dressing over top. Sprinkle with fresh herbs of choice. I used thyme.

Cranberry - Strawberry Field Green Salad

1 cup sliced, toasted almonds
6 cups mixed field greens
1 cup crumbled blue cheese
1 pint fresh strawberries, sliced
1 small purple onion, sliced
1 cup dried cranberries

Toast almonds at 300 degrees on baking sheet for 10 to 15 minutes or until browned. In a bowl, toss almonds, field greens, blue cheese, strawberries, onions and cranberries. Add vinaigrette to taste and toss again. Serves 6.

White Balsamic Vinaigrette

1/3 cup white balsamic vinegar
2/3 cups light olive oil
2 teaspoons yellow grainy mustard
3 tablespoons honey
1 shallot, finely chopped or 2 green scallions finely chopped

Process all ingredients in a processor and chill.

Corn Muffins
Biscuits
(Optional)

Heavenly Pecan Pie

4 egg whites
1 cup sugar
20 Ritz™ crackers, crushed
1 cup pecans, chopped
1 teaspoon vanilla extract

With a mixer, beat egg whites until stiff. Add sugar, and continue to beat. Add pecans, crushed crackers and vanilla. Pour into a greased 9 inch pie pan. Bake at 350 degrees for 20 minutes. Top with strawberries and whipped cream. Makes one 9 inch pie.

Tip: Fresh peaches or blueberries in season can substitute for strawberries.

Old-Fashioned Rice-Raisin Pudding

2 eggs, separated
1/2 cup white sugar
1 tablespoon butter, melted
1 teaspoon vanilla extract
½ teaspoon nutmeg
½ cup white raisins
1 ½ cups whole milk
1 cup white rice, cooked

Beat egg yolks, sugar, butter and vanilla. Add raisins, milk and rice. In a separate bowl, beat egg whites until stiff and fold into rice mixture. Bake at 325 degrees for 50 minutes or until firm. Serve with whipped cream. Serves 6 to 8.

U-PICK
Burrs Berry Farm
Since 1965

140
BOAT

When I think of seafood, I remember summers in Charleston when my children were small. They would love to go to the dock, lie down and catch crabs with bait tied to a string. We had such "memory-making times" with family and their laughter-seeing who could catch the biggest crabs.

Menu

She-Crab Soup

Wedge Salad with Zesty Honey Salad Dressing

Savannah Crab Bake

Dockside Shrimp Mornay

On the Bay Shrimp Creole

Savory Saffron Rice

Baked Cheese Grits

Deliciously Simple Asparagus Casserole

Breads

Golden Country Corn Fritters

Desserts

Lemon Meringue Pie with Brown Sugar Meringue

Lime Cheesecake

Beverages

Sweet Tea with lime, orange, lemon slices

BOAT

BOAT

Queen's Tips

Most of the dishes in this chapter can be cooked and assembled in advance allowing you more time to enjoy with your guests. Remember to try to use the freshest of seafood if possible. Lemons and limes that are fresh add color, along with unusual serving platters and trays with a seafood motif.

Recipes

She-Crab Soup

1 pound white crab meat
1 pint whole milk
1 pint light cream
½ stick butter
1 small onion, finely chopped
2 teaspoon all- purpose flour
1 teaspoon Worcestershire sauce
¼ cup sherry
Salt and pepper to taste

Sauté onion in butter until lightly browned. Add salt and pepper. Add flour, milk, cream and crab. Cook over low heat 30 minutes. Add Worcestershire sauce and sherry. Simmer 15 minutes and serve. Serves 4.

Wedge Salad with Zesty Honey Salad Dressing

1 head iceberg lettuce, divided into six wedges
8 mushrooms, sliced fine
2 medium or large tomatoes cut into wedges

Arrange on plate and drizzle with salad dressing.

Zesty Honey Salad Dressing

10 oz. mayonnaise
½ cup vegetable oil
¼ cup honey
½ teaspoon mustard
1 small onion, finely chopped
1 pinch parsley
½ lemon (juice only)
2 drops hot sauce
2 tablespoons chives, finely chopped

Mix all ingredients listed with a processor and drizzle over lettuce wedge. The dressing can be used up to 7 days if stored in a glass container and refrigerated.

Savannah Crab Bake

2 cans lump crabmeat
1 sleeve crackers, crushed (I prefer Ritz™)
2 stalks celery, minced
1 medium onion, minced
2 eggs, beaten
1 small (5 oz.) can evaporated milk
2 tablespoons mayonnaise
2 tablespoons Worcestershire sauce
½ cup butter
Salt and pepper

Sauté onion and celery in ¼ cup butter until tender. Mix in other ingredients. Place in greased casserole and sprinkle top with cracker crumbs and drizzle with remaining ¼ cup of melted butter. Bake at 450 degrees for about 15 to 20 minutes. Serves 6.

Dockside Shrimp Mornay

4 tablespoons butter or margarine
3 tablespoons onion, chopped
¼ cup all-purpose flour
½ teaspoon salt
¼ teaspoon dry mustard
Pinch of pepper
1 ½ cups whole milk
1 cup Swiss cheese, shredded
½ cup plain bread crumbs
1 lb. medium shrimp, cooked, peeled and deveined
½ cup fresh, thinly sliced mushrooms

Melt 3 tablespoons of butter in saucepan. Sauté onion. Stir in flour, salt, mustard and pepper. Add milk, cook over medium heat (stirring constantly) until sauce bubbles and thickens. Then add ¾ cup of cheese; stir until melted. Add shrimp and mushrooms to sauce. Turn into buttered six cup shallow baking dish. Combine crumbs and remaining cheese; sprinkle over top of dish. Dot with remaining 1 tablespoon butter. Bake in hot oven at 400 degrees for 15 minutes, or until sauce is bubbly and top is lightly browned. Serves 4.

On the Bay Shrimp Creole

1 large onion, chopped
½ cup green pepper, chopped
½ pound bacon, chopped
2 teaspoon Worcestershire sauce
2 teaspoons hot sauce, or to taste
Salt and pepper to taste
2 bay leaves
½ teaspoon celery seed
¼ cup chili sauce
½ cup catsup
4 cans tomato soup, undiluted
4 pounds medium shrimp,
cooked, peeled and deveined

Lightly sauté onion, green pepper and bacon. Then add all other ingredients, except shrimp. Simmer on low for 30 minutes. Add shrimp, continue cooking until heated. Serve over cooked white rice. Serves 4 to 6.

Savory Saffron Rice

2 ½ cup chicken broth
½ teaspoon salt
1 clove garlic, minced
1 cup uncooked white rice
1 tablespoon grated lemon zest
2 tablespoons fresh dill
2 tablespoons butter
2 teaspoons saffron

Bring broth to a boil and add all other ingredients. Reduce temperature to low and cook covered for 20 minutes.

Baked Cheese Grits

3 ½ cups boiling water
¾ cups regular grits
1/3 cup butter
8 oz. grated Cheddar cheese
2 eggs, beaten
1 teaspoon salt

Stir grits into boiling water and cook for 20 minutes. Remove from heat and add all other ingredients. Pour in 2 quarts greased casserole and bake at 300 degrees for 60 minutes. Serves 6.

Deliciously Simple Asparagus Casserole

1 ½ pounds fresh asparagus
16 oz. package frozen petite baby green peas
1 can cream of mushroom soup
1 can cream of celery soup
½ cup grated Cheddar cheese
½ cup slivered almonds

Steam asparagus for 5 minutes and drain. Cook peas according to package and drain. Mix soups together. Arrange all ingredients, except almonds, in layers in casserole. Sprinkle almonds on top. Bake at 350 degrees for 20 minutes. Serves 6.

Lime Cheesecake

1 ¼ cups graham crackers, crumbled
2 tablespoons sugar
¼ cup butter or margarine, melted
1 teaspoon grated lime rind
3 (8 oz.) packages cream cheese, softened
¾ cup white sugar
3 eggs
1 tablespoon grated lime zest
¼ cup Key Lime juice
1 teaspoon vanilla extract
2 cups sour cream
3 tablespoons sugar
Fresh strawberries (optional)
Lime slices (optional)

Combine first 4 ingredients; stir well. Press crumb mixture evenly over the bottom and along the sides of a 9 inch spring form pan. Bake at 350 degrees for 5 to 6 minutes. Allow to cool.

Beat cream cheese until light and fluffy; gradually add ¾ cup sugar, beating well. Add eggs, one at a time, beating well after each addition. Stir in lime zest, juice and vanilla. Pour mixture into prepared pan. Bake at 375 degrees for 45 minutes or until set.

Combine sour cream and 3 tablespoons sugar; stir well, and spread evenly over cheesecake. Bake at 500 degrees for 5 minutes. Let cool to room temperature on a wire rack; chill at least 8 hours. To serve, carefully remove sides of spring form pan. If desired, garnish with strawberries and lime slices. Makes one 9 inch cheesecake.

Lemon Meringue Pie with Brown Sugar Meringue

Crust

1 cup all-purpose flour
1/3 cup + 1 tablespoon shortening
Dash of salt
3 tablespoons ice water

For the crust, add flour and salt to a bowl. Cut in shortening until crumbly. Add ice water. Stir just until moistened. Roll dough out on floured surface to fit 9 inch pie pan. Place dough in pan. Crimp the edge. To bake, pierce bottom and sides of dough in the pie plate with a fork. Bake at 400 degrees for 10 minutes or until golden brown. Set aside.

Lemon Filling

1 ½ cups white sugar
¼ cup cornstarch
½ teaspoon salt
½ cup cold water
½ cup fresh lemon juice
3 egg yolks
2 tablespoons butter
1 ½ cups boiling water
½ lemon peel, grated
1(9 inch) baked pie crust

In saucepan combine sugar, cornstarch, and salt. Blend in cold water and lemon juice. Stir in egg yolks. Add butter and boiling water. Bring to boil over medium heat stirring constantly. Reduce heat and boil 1 minute. Stir in lemon peel. Remove from heat and pour into baked pie crust. Top with brown sugar meringue and bake at 275 degrees for 20 minutes.

Brown Sugar Meringue

4 egg whites
¼ cup cream of tartar
8 tablespoons brown sugar

In a large bowl, with mixer, beat egg whites with cream of tartar until foamy. Gradually add brown sugar and beat until stiff peaks form. Makes one 9 inch pie.

Breads

Golden Country Corn Fritters

1 1/3 cups sifted white all-purpose flour
1 ½ teaspoons baking powder
1 teaspoon salt
1 (17 oz.) can cream-style corn
1 egg, slightly beaten
2 cups vegetable oil

Sift together flour, baking powder and salt. Mix corn and egg; add to dry ingredients, stirring lightly. Heat vegetable oil in a large skillet over medium high heat. Drop batter by tablespoons into corn oil one layer at a time. Fry about 2 minutes on each side or until golden brown. Drain on absorbent paper. Sprinkle with powdered sugar for an extra special look! Serves 6 to 8.

DEEP BLUE GREEN
RYNNE CHINA CO.
WATER GREEN
CHARTREUSE
SOFT ROSE
RYNNE CHINA CO.
ANTIQUE GREEN

The Art of Hors d' Ouevres

Serve guests at your next gathering by starting the party with your special hors d'oeuvres. Take time and thought to make your food tasty, beautiful and simple. Many of us are visual and eat with our eyes! Food often tastes good because it looks as though it would be tasty.

It is a perfect opportunity to share your special hors d'oeuvres and visit with friends. Whether it is a sunny daytime event or an elegant evening celebration, orchestrate every detail to impress. Remember: a conversation over hors d'oeuvres is sometimes the best conversation!

Menu

Black Bean Dip

Gazpacho Shooters

Spanakopita Bites

Green Chile Canapé

Spinach Dip with Pita Chips

Shrimp Italian

Brisket Sliders

Guacamole with Crispy Chips

Hot Cheese Pepper Delight

Applewood Smoked Bacon Dip

Onion Cheese Dip

Cheese Spinach Tarts

Queen's Tips

Most dips can be made and assembled the day before they are to be served. Never be hesitant to use new ingredients. Hors d'oeuvres are just an appetizer, not a meal. Freshest of herbs garnish any simple dish; it will take it to the next level as an eye catcher. Have a few hearty hors d'oeuvres on your table. Men usually are hungry!

Recipes

Black Bean Dip

2 cans (15 oz.) black beans, drained well
½ cup red bell pepper, chopped
½ cup green bell pepper, chopped
4 scallions, chopped
1 cup white shoepeg corn
¼ cup cilantro, chopped
1 teaspoon salt
1 teaspoon pepper
1 fresh clove garlic, crushed
3 tablespoons lemon juice or lime juice
1 teaspoon cumin
1 jalapeño pepper, chopped (use ½ for mild)
or whole pepper for more heat.

Mix together. Serve with chips of choice. Serves 6.

Gazpacho Shooters

1 onion, quartered
1 cucumber, peeled and cored
1 bell pepper, seeded
6 to 8 tomatoes, chopped
1 quart tomato juice
4 tablespoons olive oil
¼ cup lemon juice
Dash of hot sauce
Salt and pepper to taste
Lemon slices
Parsley, chopped

In a food processor or blender, mix onion, cucumber, bell pepper and tomatoes. Add tomato juice, oil, lemon juice, hot sauce, salt and pepper. Process until no large pieces remain. Let stand at room temperature 3 hours, to blend flavors. Chill 6-24 hours. Garnish with lemon slices and chopped parsley at serving time. Serve ice cold. Serves 6 to 8.

Spanakopita Bites

1 package phylo dough
1 ½ stick butter, melted

Spinach Filling

2 packages frozen chopped spinach, thawed and drained
¾ pound Munster cheese, grated
¾ pound American cheese, grated

3 eggs
1 cup whole milk

Brush a 9 x 13 inch pan with butter (use pastry brush). Layer ½ of dough –2 sheets at a time– brush with butter. Mix cheese with spinach and spread evenly over dough. Layer remaining dough, spread with butter. Blend eggs and milk, and pour over top of dough. Cut before baking into squares. *(Must be refrigerated overnight.)* Bake at 350 degrees for 1 hour. Allow to rest before serving. Serves 8.

Green Chile Canapé

2 cups (8 oz.) Monterey Jack cheese, grated
5 eggs
1 small can green chilies (1/4 oz.) drained
2 tablespoons butter or margarine, melted
¼ cup flour
½ teaspoon baking powder
8 oz. carton cream-style cottage cheese

With mixer, combine all ingredients and mix well. Pour into greased and floured 9 x 13 inch pan. Bake at 400 degrees for 10 minutes. Reduce to 350 degrees for 20 to 30 minutes or until set. Serves 8 to 10.

Spinach Dip with Pita Chips

1 package frozen chopped spinach, thawed and well-drained
1 cup mayonnaise
1 tablespoon lemon juice
1 cup sour cream
¼ cup chopped parsley
¼ cup chopped green onion.

Mix together, chill and serve. Serves 4.

Shrimp Italian

2 pounds, fresh shrimp (medium or large), cooked, peeled and deveined

Marinate overnight using:
1 teaspoon minced garlic
1 recipe of Italian salad dressing package
1 onion, chopped

Drain and serve on platter. Garnish with lemons and limes. Serves 6 to 8.

Brisket Sliders

1 (4 to 6) pound beef brisket roast
1 medium bottle chili sauce
2 bay leaves, crumbled
1 small onion, sliced thin
1 medium jar grape jelly

Spread chili sauce and grape jelly over the roast in crock pot. Add onions and bay leaves. Cook for 8 hours or until -tender when pierced with a fork. Shred and serve on slider rolls. Top with Provolone cheese. Serve warm. Serves 20.

Guacamole with Crispy Chips

4 large, ripe avocados
Juice of 1 to 2 fresh limes
1 to 2 jalapeño peppers
1 medium onion, chopped
½ cup fresh cilantro, chopped
1 clove fresh minced garlic
Salt to taste

Halve avocados and remove seeds. Using a spoon, scoop avocado into bowl. Add lime juice to avocados and mash roughly with a fork. Using a spatula, fold in jalapeño peppers, chopped onion, cilantro, and salt. Check seasonings; add more lime juice and salt as needed. Chill 1 hour and serve with chips. Serves 4.

Hot Cheese Pepper Delight

1 (8 oz) cream cheese
6 oz. hot pepper jelly

Place cream cheese on tray. Spoon pepper jelly on top of the cream cheese. Serve with a hard cracker. Serves 4. Simple and delicious!

Applewood Smoked Bacon Dip

1 (8 oz.) package cream cheese
½ cup mayonnaise
1 cup Monterey Jack cheese, grated
2 tablespoons scallions, chopped
6 slices Applewood Smoked Bacon, cooked and crumbled
1 cup club crackers

Beat the cream cheese and mayonnaise. Add Monterey Jack cheese, scallions and bacon. Pour into a greased baking pan. Crumble crackers on top. Bake at 350 degrees for 20 minutes. Serve with crackers, breads or small toast. Serves 4 to 6.

Onion Cheese Dip

1 cup onion, chopped
1 (8 oz.) cream cheese
1 cup mayonnaise
1 cup shredded Cheddar cheese

Cream the cream cheese and mix all other ingredients together. Bake at 350 degrees in a lightly greased pan for 20 to 30 minutes. Serve with pita chips or Baguette Rounds. Serves 4 to 6.

Cheese Spinach Tarts

Pastry Shells

1 package ready-made pie crust rolls
Roll open and cut with round cookie cutter. Press into ungreased mini-muffin pans.

Filling

1 package frozen spinach, chopped, thawed and drained
4 fresh basil leaves, chopped
1 cup sour cream
1 cup mayonnaise
1 ½ cups shredded Cheddar cheese

Combine all ingredients and fill pastry shells with a heaping teaspoon of mixture. Bake at 400 degrees for 15 minutes. Reduce heat to 350 degrees for 20 to 25 minutes. Cool slightly. Serves 8.

All About the Crown

It has been a long-standing family joke that I am the Queen. The "Queen of the Kitchen", that is! Some years ago, my family purchased a beautiful brooch in the shape of a crown that I wear on occasion for a laugh. It is my family's laughter that has inspired the title of my tips, "Queen's Tips" and that silly brooch that has become my logo, the crown.

-Linda

CHOCOLATE

For the Love of Chocolate!

Chocolate Lovers have one thing in common- their extraordinary taste for this delightful ingredient made from just one tiny cocoa bean. I asked my Aunt Kathryn, who is 93 years old, what three words she recalls when she hears the word "chocolate". She said, "Candy, cakes and ...mmm... just yummy!" Everyone has indulged with some sort of decadent chocolate dessert over the years and with each bite of chocolate, a memory was made.

Menu

Ricky's Chocolate Cream Pie

Chocolate Chess Pie

Chocolate Cream Cheese Spread

White Chocolate Mousse

James' Chocolate Mousse

Brownie Shortbread Cake

Chocolate Peanut Cluster Candy

Brooke Emerson's White Chocolate Dipped Strawberries

Andy's Four-Layer Chocolate Dessert

Hot Fudge Pudding Cake

Christie's Chocolate Cake

Sierra's Chocolate Chip Cookies

CHOCOLATE

Queen's Tips

Make a hit with your guests by having an all-chocolate dessert party. It's fun, delicious and different. Experiment with a grater for chocolate shavings to garnish your trays or dessert plates. Just a sprinkle on top—will add a beautiful finish to your cakes, pies and desserts. To thin chocolate, use vegetable shortening instead of water. Store all chocolate in a cool, dry place. Chocolate tastes and cooks best at room temperature. Dark chocolate is healthier than milk chocolate. Break chocolate into one-inch pieces to speed up the melting process.

Recipes

Ricky's Chocolate Cream Pie

1 cup white sugar
2 tablespoons white all-purpose flour
3 tablespoons cocoa powder
1 cup whole milk
3 large eggs, separated
1 tablespoon butter
1 teaspoon vanilla extract
1 baked pie shell
(See Lemon Meringue Pie Crust recipe)

With mixer, combine milk, egg yolk and vanilla. Add sugar, cocoa and flour. Cook over medium heat. Stirring constantly until thick. Cool and pour into a baked pie shell. Makes one 9 inch pie.

Meringue

3 egg whites
1 teaspoon Cream of Tartar
6 tablespoons white sugar

With a mixer, beat egg whites until stiff peaks form; add cream of tartar and sugar. Spread on top of pie. Bake at 275 degrees for 20 minutes until meringue is nicely browned.

Chocolate Cream Cheese Spread

1/3 cup heavy whipping cream
2 (1 oz.) squares semisweet chocolate
1 (8 oz.) cream cheese softened

Melt cream and chocolate in microwave on high for 1 ½ minutes. Cool. With mixer, beat cream cheese until fluffy. Add cooled chocolate and mix for about 2 minutes. Cover and chill until firm. Serve with crackers, fruit, scones, bread, and biscuits. Makes 1 ¼ cups.

Chocolate Chess Pie

3 eggs
1 stick of butter
4 tablespoons cocoa powder
1 tablespoon vanilla extract
1 ¼ cups white sugar
½ cup heavy cream

1 unbaked pie crust (See Quick Pie Crust recipe.)

With a mixer, beat all ingredients together until well blended. Pour into unbaked pie crust. Bake at 350 degrees for 35 minutes. Top with whipped cream and fresh mint. Serves 8.

White Chocolate Mousse

2 (6 oz.) packages white chocolate baking bars, chopped
¼ cup whole milk
1 teaspoon vanilla extract
3 egg whites
¼ teaspoon salt
1 cup heavy whipping cream

Combine baking bars and milk in a metal mixing bowl over hot (not boiling) water; stir until baking bars are melted and mixture is smooth. Stir in vanilla extract. Transfer mixture to large bowl; set aside 15 minutes.

In medium mixer bowl, combine egg whites and salt; beat until stiff peaks form. Gently fold egg whites into chocolate mixture.

In medium mixer bowl, beat cream until stiff peaks form. Gently fold into egg white mixture. Spoon mousse into individual serving dishes. Refrigerate until ready to serve.
Makes 8 servings.

James' Chocolate Mousse

½ cup white sugar
2/3 cup water
3 cups heavy cream
1 (12 oz.) semi-sweet chocolate chips
6 egg yolks

Boil sugar and water for 3 minutes to make syrup. Whip heavy cream in food processor, and refrigerate in chilled metal bowl. Process chocolate chips in food processor. Pour in warm syrup. Add egg yolks and process until thick. Fold in heavy cream. Serve in chocolate cups or trifle bowl. Chill. Serves 8 to 10.

Brownie Shortbread Cake

2 cups white sugar
2 cups white all-purpose flour
1 teaspoon baking soda
2 teaspoon cinnamon
2 sticks margarine
4 tablespoons cocoa
1 cup water
½ cup buttermilk
2 eggs
1 teaspoon vanilla

Combine sugar, flour, baking soda and cinnamon. Set aside. Melt together the remainder of the ingredients. Pour over dry ingredients and mix well. Bake in a lightly greased 16 x 11 inch jelly roll pan at 400 degrees for 20 minutes. Serves 8.

Frosting

1 stick margarine
4 tablespoons cocoa
6 tablespoons buttermilk
1 box powdered sugar
1 teaspoon vanilla
1 cup chopped nuts

In a sauce pan, combine and bring to a boil margarine, cocoa and buttermilk. Add one box of powdered sugar and 1 teaspoon vanilla. Spread frosting on cake, and sprinkle nuts on top.

Chocolate Peanut Cluster Candy

12 ounces semisweet chocolate chips
12 ounces unsalted, dry-roasted peanuts

Melt chocolate in a microwave oven on high about 1 ½ minutes, until smooth. Stir in peanuts. Drop by teaspoonfuls onto a wax paper-lined baking pan. Refrigerate until set, 30 to 60 minutes. Cover and keep refrigerated until serving time.

Brooke Emerson's White Chocolate Dipped Srawberries

1 quart strawberries, washed and dried
1 package chocolate bark
1 package white chocolate bark

Melt chocolate bark in microwave and stir until smooth. First dip strawberries in dark chocolate and place on wax paper to harden. Then, melt white chocolate and dip strawberries only on bottom. Chill. Beautiful!

Andy's Four-Layer Chocolate Dessert

Mix together:
1 cup white all-purpose flour
1 stick butter
½ cup finely chopped nuts

Press into a 9 x 13 inch pan. Bake 15 minutes at 375 degrees. Cool.

Mix:
1 package (8 oz.) cream cheese
1 cup powdered sugar
1 cup whipped topping,
(use large carton)

Spread over crust.

Mix 2 small packages of instant chocolate pudding with 4 cups of milk. Spread over cheese mixture. Top with remainder of whipped topping in carton. Sprinkle with nuts. Serves 8 to 10.

Hot Fudge Pudding Cake

1 cup white self-rising flour
1 ¾ cup white sugar, divided
4 tablespoons cocoa powder, divided
½ cup whole milk
2 tablespoons butter, melted
1 teaspoon vanilla extract
1 ½ cups hot water
Whipped cream or vanilla ice cream

With mixer, mix flour, ¾ cup sugar, 2 tablespoons cocoa, milk, butter, and vanilla extract. Pour into 9 inch square pan. Combine 1 cup sugar, 2 tablespoons cocoa. Sprinkle over batter. Pour hot water on top. Bake at 350 degrees for 30 minutes. Serve warm with ice cream or whipped cream. Makes 6 servings.

Christie's Chocolate Cake

1 package chocolate cake mix (Swiss or Dark)
1 package instant chocolate pudding
1 ½ cups chocolate chips
1 ¾ cups sour cream
¾ cup vegetable oil
½ cup warm water
4 eggs

Mix dry ingredients. Add remainder of ingredients and mix well. Pour into greased Bundt pan. Bake at 350 degrees for 45 to 60 minutes. Cool to room temperature. Frost with an all butter frosting.

Frosting

1 stick unsalted butter
2/3 cup cocoa powder
1 (32 ounce) box powdered sugar
1/3 cup evaporated milk

With mixer, cream butter. Add cocoa, sugar and milk, mixing well until spreadable. TIP: If you prefer a large amount of frosting, double this recipe.

Sierra's Chocolate Chip Cookies

½ cup butter
½ cup shortening
¾ cup white sugar
¾ cup light brown sugar
1 teaspoon vanilla extract
2 eggs
2 ¼ cups white all-purpose flour
1 teaspoon baking soda
1 (12 oz.) package semisweet chocolate chips
1 cup chopped nuts (pecans or walnuts)

Cream butter, shortening, sugars and vanilla until fluffy. Add eggs and mix well. Gradually add flour and baking soda. Mix well. Stir in chocolate chips and nuts. Drop by a teaspoon full on ungreased cookie sheet. Bake at 375 degrees for 10 minutes. Makes 4 dozen cookies.

CHOCOLATE

LIGHTING INSTRUCTIONS

DOVER NASCAR SPRINT CUP PRACTICE
FASTEST TIME
8 55 MARTIN
23.215
9 9 AMBROSE
23.227
10 5 KAHNE
23.242
NAPA
CAMRY

Guys and Grills

Grilling is casual, easy and relaxing. Men of all ages love to grill. My three sons as well as my son-in-law certainly let grilling bring out the laughter, great foods, and memorable conversation with each other. Remember: "Don't Burn the Meat!"

Menu

Sassy Salsa Chicken with Mango Salsa Sauce

Peppercorn Filets with Blue Cheese Butter on Top

Nestor's Pan Seared Filet of Fish

Andra's Avocado and Tomato Salad

Black Bean and Wild Rice Salad

Parmesan Vinaigrette

Adam's Brussel Sprouts with Applewood Smoked Bacon

Twice Baked Potatoes

Colton's Four Cheese Macaroni and Cheese

Breads

Jalapeño Corn Bread

Desserts

Blueberry Crisp

Apple Crisp with Ice Cream

As a host, stick with your best dish if you have one you like to grill. Try out new, easy recipes on your family first before preparing them for your guests. After removing from grill, allow meat to rest before cutting to seal in the juices. Try to include your family monogram on cocktail, lunch or dinner linens! It adds a special, personal touch to your table.

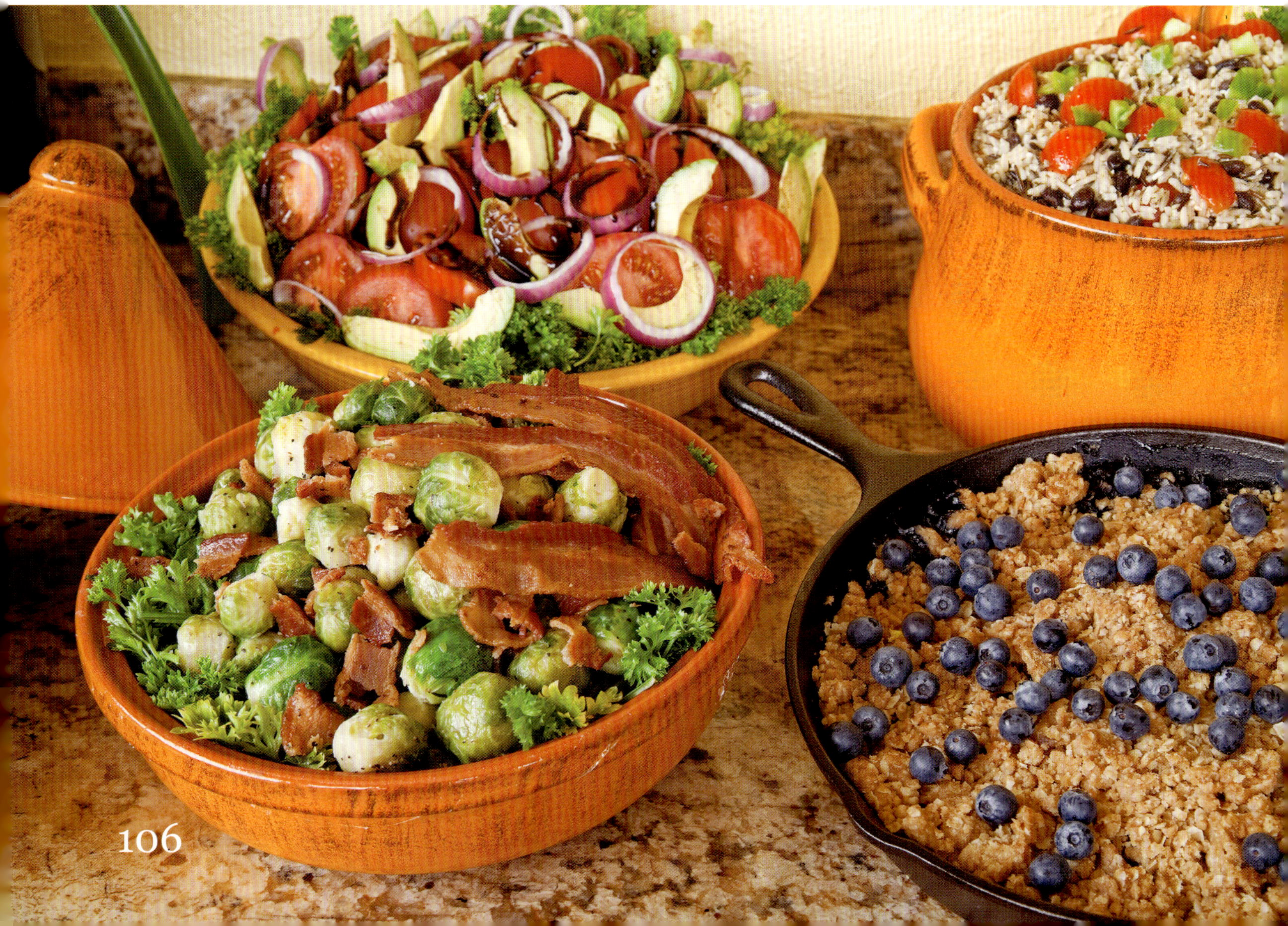

Recipes

Sassy Salsa Chicken with Mango Salsa Sauce

4 to 6 boneless, skinless chicken breasts
½ cup lite olive oil
½ cup fresh lemon juice
1 teaspoon lite salt
1 teaspoon white pepper
2 teaspoons fresh scallions or onion powder
½ teaspoon thyme
1 clove garlic, crushed or diced
½ teaspoon paprika

Marinate overnight and grill.

Mango Salsa

1 ripe mango, peeled and cut into ¼ inch dice
¼ cup fresh cilantro, minced
½ sweet onion, finely diced
1 small red pepper, diced
½ Jalapeño pepper, seeded and finely minced
3 tablespoons vegetable oil
Juice of 1 lime
½ teaspoon salt
½ teaspoon ground cumin
¼ teaspoon cayenne pepper

Mix and allow several hours for flavors to blend. Spoon over grilled chicken breast.

Peppercorn Filets with Blue Cheese Butter on Top

4 to 6 Tenderloin Filets
Seasoning of choice
(examples: salt, pepper, garlic)

Place meat on grill. Cook on grill until desired doneness.

Blue Cheese Butter

1 cup unsalted butter, softened
4 oz. package Blue cheese

Combine and spoon over filets just before removing from grill.

Nestor's Pan Seared Filet of Fish

4 (6-ounce) fish filets: red snapper, yellow tail or grouper, skin on and scales removed
½ cup all-purpose flour
1 teaspoon coarse salt, divided
½ teaspoon ground black pepper, divided
1/3 cup vegetable oil
Garnish: chopped green onions, capers, lemon slices, radish slices, fresh parsley, fresh dill

Dredge filets in flour, shaking off excess. Divide salt and pepper evenly among filets. Heat a large ovenproof skillet over high heat just until it begins to smoke. Add oil, heat until hot but not smoking. Place filets, skin sides down, in skillet. Cook, without moving, until skins are golden brown, about 4 to 5 minutes per side, lowering heat if necessary to keep from burning. Turn filets over, and cook for an additional 4 to 5 minutes. Place skillet on grill and cook with the cover down for 5 minutes. Remove, garnish and serve.

Andra's Avocado and Tomato Salad

2 large avocados, peeled and cut into bite size pieces
2 large red tomatoes, quartered
1 purple onion, sliced and separated into rings
2 tablespoons fresh lime juice
1 tablespoon Balsamic Glace vinegar, drizzled
2 tablespoons olive oil
Sea salt
Fresh ground coarse pepper

Cut up avocado, tomatoes and onion and put in a bowl. Mix salt, pepper, lime juice, vinegar and oil together in a separate bowl. Drizzle over avocados, tomatoes and onions. Do not toss or stir. Chill. Serves 6.

Black Bean and Wild Rice Salad

3 cups chicken stock
½ teaspoon coarse salt
1 cup wild rice
½ cup chopped tomatoes
3 tablespoons chopped fresh parsley
1 (10 oz.) can black beans, drained
Garnish: fresh parsley leaves
and caper berries

In a medium saucepan, combine stock and salt. Bring to a boil over high heat. Add rice, and stir to combine. Reduce heat to low; cover and simmer for 45 minutes to 1 hour. Remove from heat and drain any excess liquid; cool. In a medium bowl, combine cooked rice, tomatoes, parsley and black beans. Add Parmesan Vinaigrette (see recipe below) and stir to combine. Garnish with parsley leaves and caper berries, if desired. Prepared salad can be stored and refrigerated in an airtight container for up to 3 days. Serves 8.

Parmesan Vinaigrette

¾ cup vegetable oil
¼ cup champagne vinegar
¼ cup finely grated Parmesan
1 ½ teaspoons sugar
½ teaspoon coarse salt
¼ teaspoon ground black pepper
¼ teaspoon dry ground mustard
1/8 teaspoon cayenne pepper

In a small bowl, whisk together oil and vinegar. Add cheese, sugar, salt, black pepper, mustard and cayenne pepper.

Adam's Brussel Sprouts with Applewood Smoked Bacon

1 pound brussel sprouts
2 tablespoons butter
½ teaspoon sea salt
1 teaspoon fresh pepper
4 slices applewood smoked bacon, fried

Make a boat with foil and add ½ cup water. Wrap brussel spouts in foil and dot with butter, salt and pepper. Seal the foil. Place on grill, and cook approximately 20 to 25 minutes or until tender. Remove from foil and place in a serving dish. Sprinkle crumbled bacon on top. Season to taste. Serves 4 to 6.

Twice Baked Potatoes

6 large potatoes for baking, washed
1 teaspoon salt
¼ cup butter
½ cup whole milk
½ cup shredded cheddar cheese

Bake potatoes at 400 degrees for 60 minutes. Cut off the top of each potato. Scoop out the inside. Add butter, salt, pepper and milk. With a mixer, beat until fluffy. Fill potato shells with filling. Sprinkle cheese on top. Return to oven and bake at 375 degrees for 15 to 20 minutes or until browned. Serves 6.

Colton's Four Cheese Macaroni and Cheese

8 oz. (1/2 package) elbow macaroni
¼ cup margarine or butter
3 tablespoons all-purpose flour
1/2 teaspoon dry mustard
1/8 teaspoon salt (optional)
1/8 teaspoon black pepper
2 cups whole milk
2 cups (8 oz.) shredded Four Cheese

Cook elbow macaroni for 9 minutes. Drain, cover and set aside. Preheat oven to 350 degrees. In a medium saucepan, melt margarine or butter; blend in flour, mustard, salt and pepper. Cook until mixture is smooth and bubbly; gradually add milk. Cook and stir over medium heat until mixture boils; simmer 1 minute, stirring constantly. Gradually mix in the cheese. Stir over low heat until cheese is melted. Add pasta; mix together lightly. Pour into a greased two- quart casserole. Bake for 25 minutes. Serves 6.

Breads

Jalapeño Corn Bread

1 cup yellow corn meal
1 cup cream style corn
1 cup grated Cheddar cheese
½ cup vegetable oil
½ cup buttermilk
1 teaspoon baking soda
½ teaspoon salt
2 eggs, beaten
2 Jalapeño peppers, chopped fine
2 tablespoons bacon drippings, or oil

Mix all ingredients in a bowl except for the bacon drippings. Put bacon drippings in a 9 x 9 inch pan or preferably a black skillet. Heat in oven until drippings cover bottom of pan. Pour batter into pan, and bake for 20 to 25 minutes in a 400 degree oven. Serves 6.

Desserts

Blueberry Crisp

4 cups fresh or frozen unsweetened blueberries
1 cup packed dark brown sugar
¾ cup flour
¾ cup old-fashioned oats
½ cup (1 stick) butter, melted

Spread the blueberries in a 9 x 9 inch baking pan. Combine the brown sugar, flour and oats in a bowl and mix well. Stir in the butter. Spoon the crumb mixture over the blueberries. Bake at 350 degrees for 45 minutes. Serve warm in a dessert bowls or goblets. Serves 8. TIP: I used a black cast-iron skillet.

Apple Crisp with Vanilla Ice Cream

Crust

1 cup all-purpose flour
1/3 cup + 1 tablespoon shortening
Dash of salt
3 tablespoons ice water

Filling

4 Rome apples or Fuji apples
5 Granny Smith apples
1 cup white sugar
3 tablespoons butter
1 ½ teaspoons cinnamon
1/3 cup all-purpose flour

Crumb Toppimg

½ cup flour
¼ cup butter
¼ cup white sugar

For the crust, add flour and salt to a bowl. Cut in shortening until crumbly. Add ice water. Stir just until moistened. Roll dough out on floured surface to fit 9 inch pie pan. Place dough in pie pan. Set aside. Core, peel and slice apples and place in bowl. Toss with sugar, cinnamon and flour. Spoon into pie crust shell. Put pats of butter on top of the apples. Combine flour and sugar, cut into butter until crumbly. Sprinkle over apples. Bake at 400 degrees for 45 to 50 minutes or until done. Serves 6 to 8. Optional: Ice cream.

Happy Halloween

BOO

Spookables

Ghosts and goblins, screaming skeletons, things that go bump in the night are what we remember from our fun-filled days of trick or treating. My mother always made Halloween dinner for us fun and tasty with food that was easy to eat on the run!

We were so excited to fill our bags with candy-we hurried to eat our traditional chili she had made. Start your own tradition of ghoulish fun for your little pumpkins.

Menu

Monique's Turkey Chili with White Rice

Mini Tacos with Assorted Toppings

Ghost in a Blanket

Cinnamon Sugared Apples

Pumpkin Muffins with Pumpkin Cream Cheese

Sierra's Peanut Butter Candy Corn Cookies

Jalapeño Corn Bread

Orange Drinks

Halloween is a night when witches ride—so why not have a centerpiece of three of them huddled over a pot of chili? Decorate with spiders, cobwebs and colors of orange and black! The punch is always inviting when it is orange with spider webs cascading down the sides of your container.

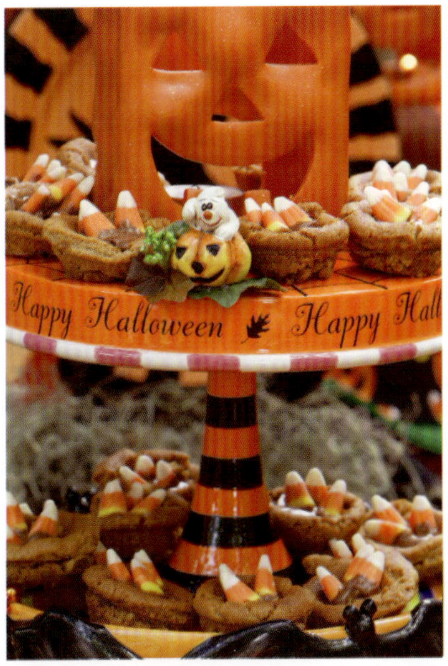

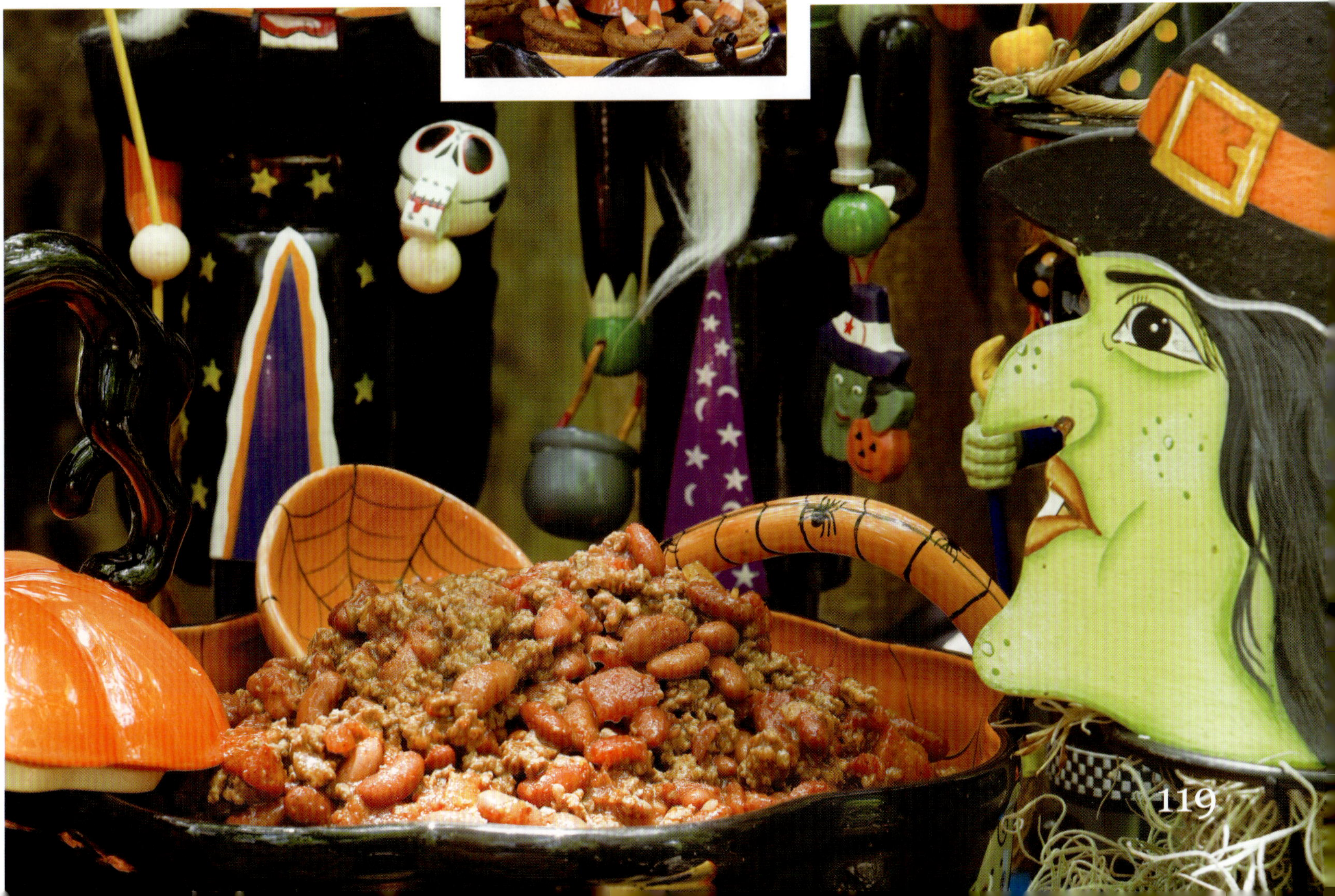

Recipes

Monique's Turkey Chili

2 tablespoons vegetable oil
1 pound ground turkey
1- 15 oz. can pinto beans, not drained
1- 15 oz.can kidney beans, not drained
2- 15 oz.cans chili beans, not drained
1- 15 oz.can crushed tomatoes
1 white onion, chopped
1 package chili mix
1 cup water
1 teaspoon salt
6 tablespoons shredded Cheddar cheese
White Rice

Heat oil in a large skillet or Dutch oven over medium high heat. Sauté turkey and onion, until turkey is evenly browned. Add pinto beans, kidney beans, chili beans and crushed tomatoes. Add water and chili mix. Cover, reduce heat and simmer on low for 20 to 30 minutes. Serve over white rice. Topped with Cheddar cheese. Makes 8 servings. Tip: You may subsitute 1 pound ground beef for turkey.

2 ½ cups chicken broth
1 cup white rice
2 tablespoons butter
½ teaspoon salt

In a saucepan, combine chicken broth, butter and salt. Bring to a boil, add white rice. Reduce heat and cook for 20 minutes or until done. Grate ½ cup fresh, raw carrot on top for orange color and crunch to serve. Serves 6.

Mini Tacos

1 package taco mix
1 package taco shells
1 pound ground beef

In a large skillet brown meat over medium high heat. Add one package taco seasoning, following directions on package. Cook until well blended. To serve, arrange mini taco shells on tray with assorted toppings. Serves 8.

Assorted Toppings

1 cup shredded lettuce
1 cup diced tomatoes
1 cup shredded Cheddar cheese
1 cup sour cream
1 cup salsa

Ghost in a Blanket

1 Package Mini Beef Lil Smokies
1 can croissants

Roll out croissants and cut in strips. Wrap each smokie with croissant dough allowing both ends of smokies to stick out. Cook according to package directions on croissants. Makes 24 bite size servings.

Tip: Kids love these! Just their size.

Cinnamon Sugar Apples

6 to 8 red and green apples
½ cup butter
¾ cup white sugar
½ cup water
3 teaspoons cinnamon

Peel, core and slice apples. Melt butter in black iron skillet; add apple slices, sugar, water and cinnamon. Simmer on low heat, covered until tender and apples are caramel-like. Serves 6.

Sierra's Candy Corn Cookies

1 (16.5 oz.) package refrigerated
Peanut butter cookie dough
Candy corn
24 Hershey's Chocolate Kiss™ candies

Shape dough into (1 inch) balls and place in lightly greased mini muffin pans. Bake at 350 degrees for 15 to 18 minutes or until lightly browned. Remove from oven and press 1 chocolate kiss into each cookie center. Top with 3 pieces of candy corn on top. Makes 24 cookies.

Pumpkin Muffins or Pumpkin Bread

2 cups white sugar
¾ cup vegetable oil
4 eggs
1 (16 oz.) can pumpkin
3 1/3 cup white all-purpose flour
2 teaspoons baking soda
½ teaspoon baking powder
1 teaspoon salt
2 teaspoons pumpkin pie spice
1 teaspoon ground nutmeg
2/3 cup water
2 teaspoons vanilla extract
1 cup chopped pecans

Combine sugar and oil, stirring well. Add eggs, one at a time, mixing well after each addition. Stir in pumpkin. Combine next 7 ingredients; add to pumpkin mixture alternately with water, beginning and ending with flour mixture. Stir in vanilla and pecans. Spoon batter into 2 lightly greased 9 x 5 x 3 inch loafpans; bake at 325 degrees for 1 hour and 10 minutes to 1 hour 20 minutes or until a wooden pick inserted in center comes out clean. Cool bread in pans 10 minutes; remove from pans and cool on wire racks. Serve with cream cheese and pumpkin spread. Yield: 2 loaves or 18 muffins.

Cream Cheese and Pumpkin Spread

1 (8oz.) package cream cheese, softened
½ cup canned pumpkin
½ teaspoon nutmeg
½ teaspoon cinnamon

With a mixer, mix until smooth cream cheese, pumpkin, nutmeg and cinnamon. Serve with pumpkin muffins or pumpkin bread.

PRODUCE OF U.S.A.
lloween
BRAND

We All Love Fall

The smell and feeling of fall is like no other. Crisp clean air, leaves turning to bright hues of red, yellow and bronze brings us all to memories of a special time in our lives. The holiday season is about to begin, whether it is a small family gathering or one with friends. "We All Love Fall!"

Menu

Ashley's Standing Rib Roast
Cornish Game Hens with
Orange Apricot Marmalade Glaze
Mixed Field Green Salad
with White Balsamic Vinaigrette
Butternut Squash Soup
Crunchy Green Beans with
Mustard Sauce
Fall Creamy Nutmeg Potatoes

Breads

Apple Butter Bread with
Honey Cheese Spread

Desserts

Linda's Crème Brulèe
Spiced Apple Cake
Warm Pumpkin Bread Pudding with
Fresh Whipped Cream
Pineapple Upside-Down Cake

Beverages

Hot Spiced Cider

Queen's Tips

Serve your individual side dishes in attractive decorative bowls; small glass, real covered pumpkins or seasonal colored dishes. Fresh fall herbs such as nutmeg, cinnamon sticks and cloves add to your designs and garnish for the season. Clove-stuffed oranges enhance your fall table with fall color and a good spiced smell. This is a great way to involve the children. They love designing their special clove oranges!

Recipes

Ashley's Sanding Rib Roast

4 ½ pound Standing Rib Roast
1 teaspoon Sea Salt
¼ cup coarsely cracked pepper

Salt and pepper top, bottom and sides of Standing Rib Roast. Place in a 9 x 13 inch roasting pan. Bake at 325 degrees for 3 hours or until the meat thermometer registers medium; 160 degrees. (For rare, bake for 2 ½ hours or until the meat thermometer registers 140 degrees.)

Cornish Game Hens with Orange Apricot Marmalade Glaze

8 Cornish game hens, cleaned
2 lemons, sliced
1 large white onion, wedged in 8 portions
2 teaspoon salt
1 teaspoon pepper
1 stick butter, melted
1 large jar orange-apricot marmalade

Rinse hens and dry, then salt and pepper. Stuff each hen with 2 lemon slices and an onion wedge. Arrange in a roasting pan. Roast covered at 375 degrees for 45 minutes to 1 hour, basting every 20 minutes with marmalade and butter. Uncover and continue to roast. Baste for 15 more minutes or longer until juices run clear and hens are golden brown. Serves 8.

Mixed Field Green Salad with White Balsamic Vinaigrette

1 cup sliced toasted almonds
1 package mixed field greens
1 cup dried cranberries
1 small purple onion, sliced into rings
1 can mandarin oranges, drained
½ cup crumbled Gorgonzola cheese on top

White Balsamic Vinaigrette

2/3 cup olive oil, extra light
1/3 cup white balsamic vinegar
3 tablespoons honey
1 teaspoon garlic, chopped
1 teaspoon grainy mustard
Optional: 1 teaspoon of lemon, lime or key lime juice

Toasted Almonds

Spread 1 cup almonds in single layer on a baking sheet. Toast at 300 degrees for 10 minutes until light brown. Combine all ingredients and toss on salad.

Tip: If dressing is refrigerated, let stand at room temperature (or microwave) for a few seconds.

Butternut Squash Soup

1 stick butter, unsalted
1 lb. butternut squash
4 red apples, peeled and diced
4 green apples, peeled and diced
4 tablespoons white sugar
1 teaspoon nutmeg
10 cups chicken broth

Melt butter and sauté chopped onion until tender. Peel and chop squash removing seeds. Add broth, apples and squash to sautéed onions. Cook until tender. Blend in a food processor to puree. Serve warm. Serve with sour cream and chopped parsley on top. Sprinkle with nutmeg. Serves 10.

Crunchy Green Beans with Mustard Sauce

2 tablespoons prepared mustard
2 tablespoons white sugar
¼ cup butter
½ teaspoon salt
3 tablespoons apple cider vinegar
2 tablespoons freshly squeezed lemon juice
2 pounds fresh green beans

Green Beans

Remove ends from green beans. Cut beans in 2-inch pieces and place in a large saucepan with boiling salted water. Cover and cook until tender but still crisp, 7 to 10 minutes. Drain and rinse under cold water to stop cooking. (May be refrigerated overnight.) Before serving the beans, prepare mustard sauce. Season to taste with salt and pepper. Serves 8.

Mustard Sauce

Combine in a small saucepan; prepared mustard, sugar, butter, salt, cider vinegar and the lemon juice. Heat slowly until the butter has melted and all the ingredients are blended. Pour over the heated green beans and keep hot until serving time.

Fall Creamy Nutmeg Potatoes

6 medium potatoes
2 cups Cheddar cheese, shredded
¼ cup butter, unsalted
1 ½ cups sour cream
½ cup green onion, chopped
1 teaspoon salt
½ teaspoon pepper
1 teaspoon ground nutmeg

Cook potatoes, drain and cool. Peel and chunk potatoes. Meanwhile, sauté onion in melted butter and add cheese until it melts. Remove from heat. Blend in sour cream, salt, pepper and potato chunks. Pour into greased casserole. Sprinkle 1 teaspoon nutmeg on top. Bake at 350 degrees for 25 minutes. Serves 6.

Breads

Apple Butter Bread with Honey Cheese Spread

½ cup butter or margarine
1 cup brown sugar
1 egg
3/4 cup buttermilk
2 teaspoons baking soda
2 cups all-purpose flour
1 teaspoon cinnamon
1 teaspoon nutmeg
1 teaspoon allspice
1 cup apple butter
½ cup pecans, chopped

Cream butter and sugar, add egg and beat well. Combine buttermilk and baking soda. Combine flour and spices, add to creamed mixture alternately with buttermilk mixture, beginning and ending with flour. Stir in apple butter and pecans. Pour into greased 9x5x3 inch loaf pan. Bake at 350 degrees for 1 hour 5 minutes or until toothpick comes out clean. Cool in pan 5 minutes. Remove to wire rack. Makes one loaf.

Honey Cheese Spread

1 cup ricotta cheese
½ cup plain yogurt
2 tablespoons honey
½ cup whipping cream

In a bowl, crumble ricotta cheese and add yogurt and honey. Mix well. Mix cream until soft peaks form. Fold into cheese mixture. Cover and chill. Will last for up to 4 days. Serve with apple butter bread.
Makes 1 ½ cups.

Desserts

Linda's Crème Brûlée

2 cups heavy whipping cream
4 egg yolks
2 tablespoons white sugar
2 tablespoons vanilla extract
4 tablespoons brown sugar

Scald heavy whipping cream and set aside to cool slightly. With a mixer, beat egg yolks, sugar and vanilla extract. Pour egg mixture into scalded cream, beating well. Pour into 6 individual buttered ramekins or custard cups. Place ramekins or custard cups into a 1 inch water bath. Bake 45 to 50 minutes at 350 degrees. Cool. Just before serving, sprinkle each serving with brown sugar and broil until sugar is melted. Serves 6.

Spiced Apple Cake

2 cups sugar
2 eggs
1 cup vegetable oil
3 cups white flour sifted
1 teaspoon salt
1 teaspoon baking soda
2 teaspoons vanilla extract
1 cup chopped nuts
3 cups chopped apples (Granny Smith, Rome, or Gala)

With a mixer, mix sugar, eggs and oil. Blend in flour, salt and baking soda. Add vanilla and mix well. Stir in nuts and apples. Pour into a greased Bundt pan or a 13 x 9 inch pan. Bake 45 minutes to 1 hour at 325 degrees. Cool. Serves 10.

Beverages

Hot Spiced Cider

1 package Mulling Spice Mix
1 gallon fresh apple cider
Cinnamon sticks (optional)

Combine in pitcher. Serve warm or cold. Garnish with cinnamon sticks. Serves 16.

Warm Pumpkin Bread Pudding with Fresh Whipped Cream

1 cup heavy cream
¾ cup canned solid-packed pumpkin
½ cup whole milk
½ cup white sugar
2 large eggs plus 1 egg yolk
¼ teaspoon salt
½ teaspoon ground cinnamon
¼ teaspoon ground ginger
5 cups French bread, crust cut off and cubed
3/4 stick unsalted butter, melted

Whisk together cream, pumpkin, milk, sugar, eggs, yolk, salt, and spices in a bowl. Toss bread cubes with butter in another bowl, add pumpkin mixture and toss to coat. Transfer to a lightly greased 8 inch square baking dish and bake until custard is set, 25 to 30 minutes. Serves 6.

Pineapple Upside-Down Cake

½ cup butter
1 cup brown sugar
1 (#2) can sliced pineapple
3 tablespoons large pecans
1 box yellow cake mix (mixed according to package directions)

Melt butter in bottom of a 9 x 13 inch pan. Spread brown sugar evenly in pan and arrange pineapple slices on sugar, filling in spaces with pecans. Pour batter over pineapple. Bake in a 375 degree oven for 35 minutes. Turn upside down on cake plate. Garnish with whipped cream. Serves 8 to 10.

It would not be the Holidays
without you joining us
for a
on
Saturday, December 3, 2011
two o'clock until five o'clock
in the afternoon ~
at the home of
Linda Ogden Epling
14800 SW 238th Street
Homestead, Florida

Sweets and Treats Christmas Exchange

Growing up in the South, I have always loved Christmas celebrations that my friends and family would have. Christmas or Holiday Sweet Exchange offers the opportunity to share traditional, delicious, and cherished recipes handed down from generation to generation. Open your home and welcome the holiday season! Celebrate, as we all remember the Blessing of this season.

It would not be the Holidays
without you joining us
for a
Christmas Sweets and Treats Exchange
on
Saturday, December 3, 2011
two o'clock until five o'clock
in the afternoon
at the home of
Linda Ogden Epling
Homestead, Florida
Bring a dozen of your favorite holiday goodies

Menu

Pineapple Cranberry Chicken Salad
on Mini Croissants or Pastry Cups
Mini Cheddar Cheese Biscuits
with Honey Ham Filling
Mini Cranberry Muffins
with Vanilla Drizzle
Mini Lemon Muffins
with Lemon Vanilla Drizzle
Fresh Coconut Fruit Salad
with Yogurt Honey Dressing

Beverages

Eggnog with Fresh Cream
and Nutmeg Sprinkle
The Queen's Spiced Cider Tea
Samovar of White Christmas Coffee
Cream and Sugar

Our memories lie in the camera's eye,
but love resides therein.

The Queen's
Spiced Cider

Queen's Tips

Ask your guests to bring a dozen of their favorite holiday goodies. Selections can be cookies, candies, bars and anything homemade and heartwarming. As a hostess, I concentrate on having something light. The guests bring the "Christmas Sweets and Treats!"

Have containers or small bags for each guest to select favorite treats from the table. Don't forget to place fresh coffee beans in a container under the coffee spout. When it drips it sends out a delicious fresh coffee smell for all to enjoy! If you are on a budget and looking for a table centerpiece, purchase inexpensive Christmas ornaments at your local store. Cascade them down the center of your table. They will be sure to catch everyone's attention. All will remember what an eye-catcher they are! Over the years, we have enjoyed sharing our family favorites with each other. You will too!

Recipes

Pineapple Cranberry Chicken Salad on Mini Croissants or Filled Pastry Cups

6 boneless, skinless chicken breasts
½ cup celery, finely chopped
½ teaspoon salt
1 cup dried cranberries
1 small can pineapple tidbits, drained
1 cup mayonnaise
¼ cup honey
Fresh parsley for garnish

Boil chicken breasts; cool and dice. Add chopped celery, salt, cranberries and pineapple to diced chicken. Mix together mayonnaise and honey. Toss with chicken mixture. Spoon mixture into pastry cups or mini croissants. Garnish with fresh parsley. Serves 10 to 12.

Pastry Cups

1 package ready-made pie crust rolls

Roll open and cut with round cookie cutter. Press into ungreased mini-muffin pans. Bake at 400 degrees for 8-10 minutes.

Mini Cheddar Cheese Biscuits with Honey Ham Filling

Honey Ham Filling

2 sticks butter or margarine
3 tablespoons prepared grainy mustard
3 tablespoons poppy seeds
1 small onion
1 teaspoon Worcestershire sauce
1 pound boiled honey ham
6 oz. Swiss cheese, grated

In a food processor, process first five ingredients. Add ham and cheese and process again. Fill cooked mini biscuits. May freeze in foil. To warm in oven, bake at 400 degrees, if thawed for 10 minutes or 20 minutes if frozen.

Cheese Biscuits

2 cups self-rising flour
1 cup buttermilk
2/3 cup shortening
½ cup shredded Cheddar cheese

Sift flour; make a well in center of flour. Add shortening to well and pour buttermilk over shortening and mix. Stir in Cheddar cheese. Roll dough out and cut into mini biscuits. Place on a greased pan. Bake at 450 degrees for 20 minutes. Makes 18.

Mini Cranberry Muffins with Vanilla Drizzle

1 ½ cups biscuit mix
1/2 cups dried cranberries
½ cup white sugar
1 egg beaten
¾ cup sour cream
1 teaspoon vanilla

Combine biscuit mix and sugar. Make well in center, add all other ingredients and mix well. Spoon into a greased mini muffin pan. Bake 12 to 15 minutes at 400 degrees or until golden. Makes 18 mini muffins.

Vanilla Drizzle

1 cup powdered sugar
3 tablespoons whole milk
½ teaspoon vanilla extract

Using a whisk, mix ingredients together and drizzle over cooked muffins.

Mini Lemon Muffins with Lemon Vanilla Drizzle

1 cup butter
1 cup sugar
4 egg yolks, beaten well
½ cup lemon juice
2 cups all purpose flour
2 teaspoon baking powder
1 teaspoon salt
4 egg whites, stiffly beaten
1 teaspoon grated lemon zest

Cream butter and sugar. Add yolks and beat until light. Add lemon juice alternately with flour, baking powder and salt. Fold in egg whites and lemon zest. Fill greased muffin tins. Bake at 375 degrees for 20 minutes.(These freeze well.)

Lemon Vanilla Drizzle

1 cup powdered sugar
3 tablespoons lemon juice

Using a whisk, mix ingredients together and drizzle over cooked muffins.

Fresh Coconut Fruit Salad with Orange Yogurt Honey Dressing

1 cup sliced strawberries
1 cup cantaloupe chunks
1 cup pineapple chunks
1 cup green or red grapes
1 cup honeydew chunks
1 cup blueberries or blackberries
1 cup raspberries for garnish
1 cup coconut, shredded

Mix together and toss lightly. Serve with Orange Yogurt Honey Dressing. Serves 6.

Orange Yogurt Honey Dressing

1 cup sour cream
1 cup vanilla yogurt
3 tablespoons of orange juice
¼ to ½ cup honey, to taste
Yields 2 ½ cups.

Whip together sour cream, yogurt and orange juice until smooth. Stir in honey. Serve over fruit.

Beverages

Eggnog with Fresh Cream and Nutmeg Sprinkle

4 egg yolks
2/3 cups white sugar
8 cups whole white milk
4 egg whites
6 tablespoons white sugar
2 teaspoon vanilla extract

1 (16oz.) whipping cream, whipped
Nutmeg sprinkled on top

With a mixer, mix sugar, egg yolks and milk. Cook over medium heat, stirring constantly until mixture coats spoon. Beat egg whites until soft peaks form. Add the 6 tablespoons of sugar. Combine with milk mixture and add vanilla. Chill mixture for 4 hours or overnight. Serve in punch bowl or pitchers topped with whip cream and nutmeg sprinkle. Serves 12. “Worth the trouble.” Delicious!

The Queen's Spiced Cider Tea

4 cups fresh apple cider
3 cups pineapple juice
2 (12oz.) frozen cranberry concentrate
2 (6 oz.) frozen orange juice concentrate
5 cups tea
8 cups club soda

Mix all ingredients and serve in punch bowl, pitchers or samovar. Float orange slices and fresh mint on top for garnish. (This beverage can be served warm or chilled.) Serves 12.

Samovar of White Christmas Coffee Cream and Sugar

Tip: Colored or decorated sugars for your holiday table will have your guests smiling sweetly! They can be purchased at local kitchen specialty stores.

Christmas
Blend
Coffee

Just for the Kids

My grandchildren wanted to add their recipes to this book. Wonderful memories have been made cooking in the kitchen with my grandchildren. I am sure you will want to share your treasured recipes and leave a legacy to the next generation from Grandma's kitchen.

Savannah's Cup of Mud

1 scoop of chocolate ice cream
1 handful of gummy worms
3 Oreos™ cookies
chocolate sauce

Put 1 scoop of chocolate ice cream in a small cup or container. Crush Oreos™ and sprinkle on top of the chocolate ice cream. Put gummy worms on top of Oreos™ and ice cream. Squirt chocolate sauce on top. Serves 1.

Queens Tips: For best results, freeze for 30 minutes before serving.

Sierra's Ants On a Log

4 celery sticks (without leaves)
½ cup peanut butter
3 tablespoons raisins

Scoop some peanut butter into the hollow part of the celery stick. Sprinkle raisins onto peanut butter evenly. Serves 2.

Queen's Tips: Use chopped apricots or cranberries instead of raisins.

Savannah's Strawberry Banana Smoothie

3 whole strawberries
1 scoop of vanilla ice cream
1 ½ of a banana
1 cup of ice cubes
2 tablespoons of honey
¾ cup of whole milk
1/3 cup of banana or strawberry yogurt

Put all ingredients in a blender. Blend like there is no tomorrow. Pour in 2 cups and serve. Serves 2.

Peanut Butter and Banana Sandwiches

1 ½ of a banana peeled and cut into pieces
2 tablespoons of peanut butter
2 slices of bread

Spread peanut butter onto bread (both sides). Lay banana slices over peanut butter evenly. Cut sandwiches with a cookie cutter into cute shapes (flowers, butterflies, stars, etc.). Serves 1.

Queen's Tips: Cut off crust before using cookie cutter.

Brooke Emerson's Peanut Butter Apple

1 apple, red or green
1 ½ teaspoon peanut butter

Core out center of apple leaving the bottom in tack. Put the peanut butter in center of apple. Chill for 30 minutes. Slice into wedges or rounds. Serves 1.

Savannah's Cheese Quesadillas

1 flour tortilla
3/4 cup of cheddar cheese
1 tablespoon butter

Melt butter in pan. Brown tortilla and put cheese on 1/2 of tortilla. Fold other half of tortilla over cheese. Brown on both sides. Cut into thirds. Serves 1.

Queen's Tips: Add chopped or cubed ham or chicken for extra flavor in quesadillas.

James and Colton's Grilled Cheese for the Boys

2 slices of white bread, crust removed
2 slices of yellow cheese
1 tablespoon of butter

Lay slices of cheese on one slice of bread. Cover with other slice. Butter both sides of bread. Put in a skillet and brown on each side. Cut into quarters or with a cute cookie cutter.

Sierra's Strawberry Shake

1 cup strawberry ice cream
1/4 cup whole milk
3 strawberries cut up

In blender place ice cream, milk and strawberries. Cover and blend. Pour into glass. Squirt with whip cream and top with cherry.

Queen's Tips

Try to have a special apron for each child. When cooking in the kitchen with children, always be sure the handle of the pot or pan is turned to the side and not hanging over the stove. Using cookie cutters in place of knives are fun and safe. Let the children share in the preparation as much as possible. It gives them confidence while having fun. Make sure you giggle a lot with them!

Index

D